Untold Windows Trick's

and Secrets

By John Albert!

About Book:

The Book "Untold Windows Trick's & Secrets"
consists of untold Window's Tricks & secrets that
allows you to customize windows according to your
will!

Introduction:

Welcome to another Hacking Truths Manual. This time I have a collection of Tips and Tricks which no body normally knows, the secrets which Microsoft is afraid to tell the people, the information which you will seldom find all gathered up and arranged in a single file. To fully reap this Manual you need to have a basic understanding of the Windows Registry, as almost all the Tricks and Tips involve this file.

****

Important Note: Before you read on, you need to keep one thing in mind. Whenever you make changes to the Windows Registry you need to Refresh it before the changes take place. Simply press F5 to refresh the registry and enable the changes. If this does not work Restart your system

****

Exiting Windows the Cool and Quick Way

Normally it takes a hell lot of time just Shutting down Windows, you have to move your mouse to the Start Button, click on it, move it again over Shut Down, click, then move it over the necessary option and click, then move the cursor over the OK button and once again (you guessed it) click.This whole process can be shortened by creating shortcuts on the Desktop which will shut down Windows at the click of a button. Start by creating a new shortcut(right click and select New> Shortcut). Then in the command line box, type (without the quotes.)

'C:\windows\rundll.exe user.exe,exitwindowsexec'

This Shortcut on clicking will restart Windows immediately without any Warning. To create a Shortcut to Restarting Windows, type the following in the Command Line box:

'c:\windows\rundll.exe   user.exe,exitwindows'

This Shortcut on clicking will shut down Windows immediately without any Warning.

Ban Shutdowns : A trick to Play on Lamers

This is a neat trick you can play on that lamer that has a huge ego, in this section I teach you, how to disable the Shut Down option in the Shut Down Dialog Box. This trick involves editing the registry, so please make backups. Launch regedit.exe and go to :

HKEY_CURRENT_USER\Software\Microsoft\Windows\CurrentVersion \Policies\Explorer

In the right pane look for the NoClose Key. If it is not already there then create it by right clicking in the right pane and selecting New > String Value.(Name it NoCloseKey) Now once you see the NoCloseKey in the right pane, right click on it and select Modify. Then Type 1 in the Value Data Box.

Doing the above on a Win98 system disables the Shut Down option in the Shut Down Dialog Box. But on a Win95 machine if the value of NoCloseKey is set to 1 then click on the Start > Shut Down button displays the following error message:

This operation has been cancelled due to restrictions in effect on this computer. Please contact your system administrator.

You can enable the shut down option by changing the value of NoCloseKey to 0 or simply deleting the particular entry i.e. deleting NoCloseKey.

Instead of performing the above difficult to remember process, simply save the following with an extension of .reg and add it's contents to the registry by double clicking on it.

REGEDIT4

[HKEY_CURRENT_USER\Software\Microsoft\Windows\ CurrentVersio n\Policies\Explorer]

"NoClose"="1"

Disabling Display of Drives in My Computer

This is yet another trick you can play on your geek friend. To disable the display of local or networked drives when you click My Computer go to :

HKEY_CURRENT_USER\Software\Microsoft\Windows\ CurrentVersion \Policies\Explorer

Now in the right pane create a new DWORD item and name it NoDrives. Now modify it's value and set it to 3FFFFFF (Hexadecimal) Now press F5 to refresh. When you click on My Computer, no drives will be shown. To enable display of drives in My Computer, simply delete this DWORD item. It's .reg file is as follows:

REGEDIT4

[HKEY_CURRENT_USER\Software\Microsoft\Windows\ CurrentVersio n\Policies\Explorer]

"NoDrives"=dword:03ffffff

Take Over the Screen Saver

To activate and deactivate the screen saver whenever you want, goto the following registry key:

HKEY_CURRENT_USER\Software\Microsoft\Windows\CurrentVersion \ScreenSavers

Now add a new string value and name it Mouse Corners. Edit this new value to -Y-N. Press F5 to refresh the registry. Voila! Now you can activate your screensaver by simply placing the mouse cursor at the top right corner of the screen and if you take the mouse to the bottom left corner of the screen, the screensaver will deactivate.

Pop a banner each time Windows Boots

To pop a banner which can contain any message you want to display just before a user is going to log on, go to the key:

HKEY_LOCAL_MACHINE\SOFTWARE\Microsoft\Windo

ws\CurrentVers ion\WinLogon

Now create a new string Value in the right pane named LegalNoticeCaption and enter the value that you want to see in the Menu Bar. Now create yet another new string value and name it: LegalNoticeText. Modify it and insert the message you want to display each time Windows boots. This can be effectively used to display the company's private policy each time the user logs on to his NT box. It's .reg file would be:

REGEDIT4

[HKEY_LOCAL_MACHINE\SOFTWARE\Microsoft\Wind ows\CurrentVer sion\Winlogon]

"LegalNoticeCaption"="Caption here."

Delete the Tips of the Day to save 5KB

Windows 95 had these tips of the day which appeared on a system running a newly installed Windows OS. These tips of the day are stored in the Windows Registry and consume 5K of space. For those of you who are really concerned about how much free space your hard disk has, I have the perfect trick.

To save 5K go to the following key in Regedit:

HKEY_LOCAL_MACHINE\Software\Microsoft\Windows\CurrentVersio n\Explorer\Tips

Now simply delete these tricks by selecting and pressing the DEL key.

Change the Default Locations

To change the default drive or path where Windows will look for it's installation files, go to the key:

HKEY_LOCAL_MACHINE\Software\Microsoft\Window

s\CurrentVersio n\Setup\SourcePath

Now you can edit as you wish.

Secure your Desktop Icons and Settings

You can save your desktop settings and secure it from your nerdy friend by playing with the registry. Simply launch the Registry Editor go to:

HKEY_CURRENT_USER\Software\Microsoft\Windows\ CurrentVersion \Policies\Explorer

In the right pane create a new DWORD Value named NoSaveSettings and modify it's value to 1. Refresh and restart for the settings to get saved.

CLSID Folders Explained

Don't you just hate those stubborn stupid icons that refuse to leave the desktop, like the Network Neighborhood icon. I am sure you want to know how you can delete them. You may say, that is really simple, simply right click on the concerned icon and select Delete. Well not exactly, you see when you right click on these special folders(see entire list below)neither the rename nor the delete option does not appear. To delete these folders, there are two methods, the first one is using the System Policy Editor(Poledit in the Windows installation CD)and the second is using the Registry.

Before we go on, you need to understand what CLSID values are. These folders, like the Control Panel, Inbox, The Microsoft Network, Dial Up Networking etc are system folders. Each system folder has a unique CLSID key or the Class ID which is a 16-byte value which identifies an individual object that points to a corresponding key in the registry.

To delete these system Folders from the desktop

simply go to the following registry key:

HKEY_LOCAL_MACHINE\Software\Microsoft\Window s\CurrentVersio n\Explorer\Desktop\Namespace{xxxxxxxx-xxxx-xxxx-xxxx-xxxxxxxxxxxx}

To delete an icon simply delete the 16 byte CLSID value within "NameSpace". The following are the CLSID values of the most commonly used icons:

My   Briefcase:{85BBD920-42AO-1069-A2E4-08002B30309D}

Desktop: {00021400-0000-0000-C000-0000000000046}

Control   Panel:{21EC2020-3AEA-1069-A2DD-08002B30309D}

Dial-Up-Networking:{992CFFA0-F557-101A-88EC-00DD01CCC48}

Fonts: {BD84B380-8CA2-1069-AB1D-08000948534}

Inbox   :{00020D76-0000-0000-C000-000000000046}

My   Computer   :{20D04FE0-3AEA-1069-A2D8-08002B30309D}

Network   Neighborhood:{208D2C60-3AEA-1069-A2D7-O8002B30309D}

Printers   :{2227A280-3AEA-1069-A2DE-O8002B30309D}

Recycle   Bin   :{645FF040-5081-101B-9F08-00AA002F954E}

The   Microsoft   Network:{00028B00-0000-0000-C000-000000000046}

History: {FF393560-C2A7-11CF-BFF4-444553540000}

Winzip   :{E0D79300-84BE-11CE-9641-444553540000}

For example, to delete the Recycle Bin, first note down it's CLSID value, which is: 645FF040-5081-101B-9F08-00AA002F954E. Now go to the Namespace key in the registry and delete the corresponding key.

HKEY_LOCAL_MACHINE\SOFTWARE\Microsoft\Windows\CurrentVers ion\explorer\Desktop\NameSpace\{645FF040-5081-101B-9F08-00AA002F954E}

Similarly to delete the History folder, delete the following key:

HKEY_LOCAL_MACHINE\SOFTWARE\Microsoft\Windows\CurrentVers ion\explorer\Desktop\NameSpace\{FBF23B42-E3F0-101B-8488-00AA003E56F8}

Sometimes, you may need to play a trick on your brother or friend, well this one teaches you how to hide all icons from the Desktop. Go to the following registry key:

HKEY_CURRENT_USER\Software\Microsoft\Windows\ CurrentVersion \Policies\Explorer

In the right pane create a new DWORD value by the name: NoDesktop and set its value to: 1. Reboot and you will find no icons on the desktop.

Till now you simply learnt how to delete the special system folders by deleting a registry key, but the hack would have been better if there was a way of adding the DELETE and RENAME option to the right

click context menus of these special folders. You can actually change the right click context menu of any system folder and add any of the following options: RENAME, DELETE, CUT, COPY, PASTE and lots more.

This hack too requires you to know the CLSID value of the system folder whose menu you want to customize. In this section, I have taken up Recycle Bin as the folder whose context menu I am going to edit.

Firstly launch the registry editor and open the following registry key:

HKEY_CLASSES_ROOT\CLSID\{645FF040-5081-101B-9F08-00AA002F954E}\ShellFolder.

In Case you want to edit some other folder like say the FONTS folder, then you will open the following key:

HKEY_CLASSES_ROOT\CLSID\{CLSID VALUE HERE}\ShellFolder.

In the right pane there will be a DWORD value names attributes. Now consider the following options:

To add the Rename option to the menu, change the value of Attributes to

50 01 00 20

To add the Delete option to the menu, change the value of Attributes to

60 01 00 20

3. To add both the Rename & Delete options to the menu, change the value of Attributes to 70,01,00,20

4. Add Copy to the menu, change Attributes to 41 01 00 20

5. Add Cut to the menu, change Attributes to 42 01 00 20

6. Add Copy & Cut to the menu, change Attributes to 43 01 00 20

7. Add Paste to the menu, change Attributes to 44 01 00 20

8. Add Copy & Paste to the menu, change Attributes to 45 01 00 20

9. Add Cut & Paste to the menu, change Attributes to
   46 01 00 20

10. Add all Cut, Copy & Paste to the menu, change Attributes to 47 01 00 20

We want to add only the Rename option to the right click context menu of the Recycle Bin, so change the value of attributes to: 50 01 00 20. Press F5 to refresh and then after rebooting you will find that
when you right click on the Recycle Bin a RENAME option pops up too.

To reset the default Windows options change the value of Attributes back to

40 01 00 20

The Registry File which one can create for the above process would be something like the below:

REGEDIT4

[HKEY_CLASSES_ROOT\CLSID\{645FF040-

5081-101B-9F08-00AA002F954E}\Shell-Folder]

"Attributes"=hex:50,01,00,20

To access say the Modem Properties in the Control Panel Folder, the normal procedure is: Click on Start, Click on Settings> Control Panel and then wait for the Control Panel window to pop up and then ultimately click on the Modems icon.

Wouldn't it be lovely if you could shorten the process to: Click on Start> Control Panel>Modems. Yes you can add the Control Panel and also all other Special System Folders directly to the first level Start Menu. Firstly collect the CLSID value of the folder you want to add to the start menu. I want to add Control Panel hence the CLSID value is: 21EC2020-3AEA-1069-A2DD-08002B30309D

Now right click on the Start Button and select Open. Now create a new folder and name it: Control   Panel.{21EC2020-3AEA-1069-A2DD-08002B30309D}

NOTE: Do not forget the period after the 'l' in Panel. Similarly all system folders can be added to the Start Menu.(accept My Briefcase, I think)

Deleting System Options from the Start menu

You can actually remove the Find and Run options from the start menu by performing a simple registry hack. Again like always Launch the registry editor and scroll down to the below key:

HKEY_CURRENT_USER\Software\Microsoft\Windows\ CurrentVersion \Policies\Explorer

Right-click on the right pane and select New, DWORD Value. Name it NoFind.(To remove the RUN option name it NoRun). Double-click the newly create DWORD to edit it's value and enter 1 as its value. This will disable the FIND option of the Start Menu and will also disable the default Shortcut key(F3 for Find.)

To restore the Run or find command modify the value of the DWORD to 0 or simply Delete the DWORD value.

Fed Up of the boring Old Yellow Folder Icons?[Drive Icons Included]

NOTE: This trick hasn't been tried on Win98.

You can easily change the boring yellow folder icons to your own personalized icons. Simply create a text file and copy the following lines into it:

[.ShellClassInfo]

ICONFILE=Drive:\Path\Icon_name.extension

Save this text file by the name, desktop.ini in the folder, whose icon you want to change. Now to prevent this file from getting deleted change it's attributes to Hidden and Read Only by using the ATTRIB command.

To change the icon of a drive, create a text file containing the following lines:

[Autorun]

ICON=Drive:\Path\Icon_name.extension

Save this file in the root of the drive whose icon you want to change and name it autorun.inf For Example, if you want to change the icon of a floppy, SAVE THE icon in a:\icon_name.ico One can also create a kewl icon for the Hard Disk and create a text file [autorun.inf] and store it in "c:\".

Securing NT

By default, NT 4.0 displays the last person who logged onto the system. This can be considered to be a security threat, especially in the case of those who choose their password to be same as their Username. To disable this bug which actually is a feature, go to the following key in the registry editor:

HKEY_LOCAL_MACHINE\Software\Microsoft\WindowsNT\CurrentVer sion\Winlogon

Click and select the ReportBookOK item and create a new string value called DontDisplayLastUserName. Modify it and set it's value to 1.

As a system administrator, you can ensure that the passwords chosen by the users are not too lame or too easy to guess. NT has this lovely utility called the User Manager which allows the administrator to set the age limit of the password which forces the users to change the password after a certain number of days. You can also set the minimum length of passwords and prevent users to use passwords which already have been used earlier and also enable account lockouts which will deactivate an account after a specified number of failed login attempts.

When you log on to Win NT, you should disable Password Caching, this ensures Single NT Domain login and also prevents secondary Windows Logon screen.

Simply copy the following lines to a plain text ASCII editor like: Notepad and save it with an extension, .reg

----------------DISABLE.reg----------------

REGEDIT4

[HKEY_LOCAL_MACHINE\SOFTWARE\Microsoft\Wind ows\CurrentVer sion\Policies\Network]

"DisablePwdCaching"=dword:00000001

----------------DISABLE.reg----------------

To Enable Password Caching use the following .reg file:

--------------Enable.reg----------------

REGEDIT4

[HKEY_LOCAL_MACHINE\SOFTWARE\Microsoft\Wind ows\CurrentVer sion\Policies\Network]

"DisablePwdCaching"=dword:00000000

--------------Enable.reg----------------

Cleaning Recent Docs Menu and the RUN MRU

The Recent Docs menu can be easily disabled by editing the Registry. To do this go to the following Key:

HKEY_CURRENT_USER\Software\Microsoft\Windows\ CurrentVersion \Policies\Explorer

Now in the right pane, create a new DWORD value by the name: NoRecentDocsMenu and set it's value to 1. Restart Explorer to save the changes.

You can also clear the RUN MRU history. All the listings are stored in the key:

HKEY_USERS\.Default\Software\Microsoft\Windows\ CurrentVersion\ Explorer\RunMRU

You can delete individual listings or the entire listing. To delete History of Find listings go to:

HKEY_CURRENT_USER\Software\Microsoft\Windows\ CurrentVersion\Explorer\Doc Find Spec MRU and delete.

Customizing the Right Click Context Menu of the Start Menu

When you right click on the start menu, only 3 options pop up: Open, Explore, and Find. You can add your own programs to this pop up menu(which comes up when we right click on it.) Open Regedit and go to the following registry key:

HKEY_CLASSES_ROOT\Directory\Shell

Right click on the shell and create a new Sub Key (You can create a new SubKey by right clicking on the Shell Key and selecting New > Key.). Type in the name of the application you want to add to the start menu. I want to add Notepad to the Start Menu and hence I name this new sub key, Notepad. Now right click on the new registry key that you just created and create yet another new key named Command. Enter the full path of the application, in this case Notepad in the default value of Command in the right pane. So I Modify the value of the default string value and enter the full pathname of Notepad:

c:\wndows\notepad.exe.

Now press F5 to refresh. Now if you right click on the Start Button you will find a new addition to the Pop Up Menu called Notepad. Clicking on it will launch Notepad.

We can not only add but also remove the existing options in this pop up box.

To delete the Find option, go to the following registry key:

HKEY_CLASSES_ROOT\Directory\Shell\Find

Delete Find. DO NOT delete Open else you will not be able to open any folders in the Start Menu like Programs, Accessories etc.

BMP Thumbnail As Icon

You can actually change the default BMP icon to a

thumbnail version of the actual BMP file. To do this simply go to HKCU\Paint.Picture\Default. In the right pane change the value of default to %1. Please note however that this will slow down the display rate in explorer if there are too many BMP thumbnails to display. You can use other icons too, simply enter the pathname.To restore back to the normal change the vale of default back to: C:\Progra~1\Access~1\MSPAINT.EXE,1.

Customizing the Shortcut Arrow

All shortcuts have a tiny black arrow attached to it's icon to distinguish from normal files. This arrow can sometimes be pretty annoying and as a Hacker should know how to change each and everything, here goes another trick. Launch the Registry Editor and go to:

HKEY_LOCAL_MACHINE\SOFTWARE\Microsoft\Windows\CurrentVers ion\explorer\Shell Icons.

Now, on the right pane is a list of icons (we found out that on some systems, Windows 98 especially, the right pane is blank. Don't worry, just add the value as required). Find the value 29. If it isn't there, just add it. The value of this string should be C:\Windows\system\shell32.dll, 29 (which means the 30th icon in shell32.dll - the first one begins with 0). Now, we need blank icon to do this. Just create one with white as the whole icon. Go here to learn how to create an icon. Once done just change the value to C:\xxx.ico, 0 where "xxx" is the full path of the icon file and "0" is the icon in it.

Now for some fun. If the blank icon is a bit boring, change it again. You will find that under shell32.dll there is a gear icon, a shared folder (the hand) and much more. Experiment for yourself!

Use Perl to Get List or Services Running on your NT box

Use the following Perl Script to get a list of Services running on your NT system

--------------script.pl-----------------

```
#!c:\per\bin\perl.exe
```

```perl
use Win32::Service;

my ($key, %service, %status, $part);


Win32::Service::GetServices(' ',\%services);

foreach $key (sort keys %services) {

print    "Print    Name\t:    $key,
$services{$key}\n";
Win32::Service::GetStatus(        '
',$services{$key};

\%status);

foreach $part (keys %status) {

print    "\t$part    :    $status{$part}\n"    if($part    eq
"CurrentState");

}


}
```

-------------script.pl-------------------

Internet Explorer Tricks and Tips

Resizable Full Screen Toolbar

The Full Screen option increases the viewable area and makes surfing more enjoyable but sometimes we need the Toolbar but also need to have extra viewing area. Now this hack teaches you how to change the size of the Internet Explorer toolbar. This registry hack is a bit complicated as it involves Binary values, so to make it simple, I have included the following registry file which will enable the resizable option of the Internet Explorer toolbar which was present in the beta version of IE.

REGEDIT4

[HKEY_CURRENT_USER\Software\Mic rosoft\Internet Explorer\Toolbar]

"Theater"=hex:0c,00,00,00,4c,00,00,00,74,00,00,00,1 8,00,00,00,1b,00,00,00,5c,\

00,00,00,01,00,00,00,e0,00,00,00,a0,0f,00,00,05,0
0,00,00,22,00,

00,00,26,00,\

00,00,02,00,00,00,21,00,00,00,a0,0f,00,00,04,00,0
0,00,01,00,00,
00,a0,0f,00,\

00,03,00,00,00,08,00,00,00,00,00,00,00

****

HACKING TRUTH: Internet Explorer 5 displays the friendly version of HTTP errors like NOT FOUND etc . They are aimed at making things easier for newbies. If you would rather prefer to see the proper error pages for the web server you're using, go to Tools, Internet Options and select the Advanced tab. Then scroll down and uncheck the Show friendly http errors box.

****

Making the Internet Explorer & the Explorer Toolbars Fancy

The Internet Explorer toolbar looks pretty simple. Want to make it fancy and kewl? Why not add a background image to it. To do this kewl hack launch the Windows Registry Editor and go to the following key: HKEY_CURRENT_USER\SOFTWARE\Microsoft\ Internet Explorer\Toolbar\.

Now in the right pane create a new String Value and name it BackBitmap and modify it's value to the path of the Bitmap you want to dress it up with by rightclicking on it and choosing Modify.

When you reboot the Internet Explorer and the Windows Explorer toolbars will have a new look.

Change Internet Explorer's Caption

Don't like the caption of Internet Explorer caption? Want to change it? Open the registry editor and go to

HKEY_LOCAL_MACHINE\SOFTWARE\Microsoft\Intern
et
Explorer\Main.

In the right pane create a new String Value
names Window Title (Note the space between
Window and Title). Right click on this newly
created String Value and select Modify. Type in
the new caption you want to be displayed. Restart
for the settings to take place.

Now let's move on to some Outlook
Express Tricks.

Colorful Background

Don't like the boring background colors of Outlook
Express? To change it launch the Windows Registry
Editor and scroll down to the

HKEY_CURRENT_USER\Software\Microsoft\Internet
Mail And News key.

On the left pane, click on ColorCycle or select Edit and Modify in the menu. Now change the value to 1. Close and restart. Now, launch Outlook Express and whenever you open up a New Message, hold down ctrl-shift and tap the z key to scroll to change the background color. Repeat the keystroke to cycle through the colors.

Internet Explorer 5 Hidden Features

Microsoft Internet Explorer 5 has several hidden features which can be controlled using the Windows Registry. Open your registry and scroll down to the following key:

HKEY_CURRENT_USER\Software\Policies\Microsoft\Internet
Explorer\Restrictions

Create a new DWORD value named x(See complete list of values of x below) and modify it's value to 1 to enable it and to 0 to disable it.

NoBrowserClose : Disable the option of closing Internet Explorer.

NoBrowserContextMenu : Disable right-click context menu.

NoBrowserOptions : Disable the Tools / Internet Options menu.

NoBrowserSaveAs : Disable the ability to Save As.

NoFavorites : Disable the Favorites.

NoFileNew : Disable the File / New command.

NoFileOpen : Disable the File / Open command.

NoFindFiles : Disable the Find Files command.

NoSelectDownloadDir : Disable the option of selecting a download directory.

NoTheaterMode : Disable the Full Screen view option.

Hacking Secrets

Almost all system administrators make certain changes and make the system restricted. System Administrators can hide the RUN option, the FIND command, the entire Control Panel, drives in My Computer like D: A: etc. They can even restrict activities of a hacker my disabling or hiding, even the tiniest options or tools.

Most commonly these restrictions are imposed locally and are controlled by the Windows Registry. But sometimes the smart system administrators control the activities of the hacker by imposing restrictions remotely through the main server.

Poledit or Policy Editor is a small kewl tool which is being commonly used by system administrators to alter the settings of a system. This utility is not installed by default by Windows. You need to install in manually from the Windows 98 Installation Kit from the Resource Kit folder. user.dat file that we saw earlier.

The Policy Editor tool imposes restrictions on the user's system by editing the user.dat file which in turn means that it edits the Windows Registry to change the settings. It can be used to control or restrict access to each and every folder and option you could ever think of. It has the power to even restrict access to individual folders, files, the Control Panel, MS DOS, the drives available etc.

Sometimes this software does make life really hard for a Hacker. So how can we remove the restrictions imposed by the Policy Editor? Well read ahead to learn more.

You see the Policy Editor is not the only way to restrict a user's activities. As we already know that the Policy Editor edits the Windows Registry(user.dat) file to impose such restrictions. So this in turn would mean that we can directly make changes to the Windows Registry using a .reg file or directly to remove or add restrictions.

Launch Regedit and go to the following Registry Key:

HKEY_CURRENT_USER/Software/Microsoft/CurrentVersion/Policies

Under this key, there will definitely be a key named explorer. Now under this explorer key we can create new DWORD values and modify it's value to 1 in order to impose the restriction. If you want to remove the Restriction, then you can simply delete the respective DWORD values or instead change

their values to 0. The following is a list of DWORD values that can be created under the Explorer Key-

:

NoDeletePrinter: Disables Deletion of already installed Printers

NoAddPrinter: Disables Addition of new Printers

NoRun : Disables or hides the Run Command

NoSetFolders: Removes Folders from the Settings option on Start Menu (Control Panel, Printers, Taskbar)

NoSetTaskbar: Removes Taskbar system folder from the Settings option on Start Menu

NoFind: Removes the Find Tool (Start >Find)

NoDrives: Hides and does not display any Drives in My Computer

NoNetHood: Hides or removes the Network Neighborhood icon from the desktop

NoDesktop: Hides all items including, file, folders and system folders from the Desktop

NoClose: Disables Shutdown and prevents the user from normally shutting down Windows.

NoSaveSettings: Means to say, 'Don't save settings on exit'

DisableRegistryTools: Disable Registry Editing Tools (If you disable this option, the Windows Registry Editor(regedit.exe) too

will not work.)

NoRecentDocsHistory: Removes Recent Document system folder from the Start Menu (IE 4 and above)

ClearRecentDocsOnExit: Clears the Recent Documents system folder on Exit.

NoInternetIcon: Removes the Internet (system folder) icon from the Desktop

Under the same key: HKEY_CURRENT_USER/Software/Microsoft/CurrentVersion/Policies you can create new subkeys other than the already existing Explorer key. Now create a new key and name it System. Under this new key, system we can create the following new DWORD values(1 for enabling the particular option and 0 for disabling the particular option):

NODispCPL: Hides Control Panel

NoDispBackgroundPage: Hides Background page.

NoDispScrsavPage: Hides Screen Saver Page

NoDispAppearancePage: Hides Appearance Page

NoDispSettingsPage: Hides Settings Page

NoSecCPL: Disables Password Control Panel

NoPwdPage: Hides Password Change Page

NoAdminPaqe: Hides Remote Administration Page

NoProfilePage: Hides User Profiles Page

NoDevMgrPage: Hides Device Manager Page

NoConfigPage: Hides Hardware Profiles Page

NoFileSysPage: Hides File System Button

NoVirtMemPage: Hides Virtual Memory Button

Similarly, if we create a new subkey named Network, we can add the following DWORD values under it(1 for enabling the particular option and 0 for disabling the particular option):

NoNetSetupSecurityPage: Hides Network Security Page

NoNelSetup: Hides or disables the Network option in the Control Panel

NoNetSetupIDPage: Hides the Identification Page

NoNetSetupSecurityPage: Hides the Access Control Page

NoFileSharingControl: Disables File Sharing Controls

NoPrintSharing: Disables Print Sharing Controls

Similarly, if we create a new subkey named

WinOldApp, we can add the following DWORD values under it(1 for enabling the particular option and 0 for disabling the particular option):

Disabled: Disable MS-DOS Prompt

NoRealMode: Disable Single-Mode MS-DOS.

So you see if you have access to the Windows Registry, then you can easily create new DWORD values and set heir value to 1 for enabling the particular option and 0 for disabling the particular option. But Sometimes, access to the Windows Registry is blocked. So what do you do? Go to the Windows Directory and delete either user.dat or system.dat (These 2 files constitute the Windows Registry.) and reboot. As soon as Windows logs in, it will display a Warning Message informing you about an error in the Windows Registry. Simply ignore this Warning Message and Press CTRL+DEL+ALT to get out of this warning message.(Do not press OK) You will find that all restrictions have been removed.

The most kind of restriction found quite commonly is the Specific Folder Restriction, in which users are not allowed access to specific folders, the most common being the Windows folder, or sometimes even access to My Computer is blocked. In effect, you simply cannot seem to access the important kewl files which are needed by you to do remove restrictions. What do you? Well use the RUN command. (START >RUN). But unfortunately a system administrator who is intelligent enough to block access to specific folder, would definitely have blocked access to the RUN command. Again we are stuck.

Windows is supposed to be the most User Friendly Operating System on earth. (At least Microsoft Says so.)

It gives the User an option to do the same thing in various ways. You see the RUN command is only the most convenient option of launching applications, but not the only way. In Windows you can create shortcuts to almost anything from a file, folder to a Web URL. So say your system administrator has blocked access to the c:\windows\system folder and you need to access it. What do you do? Simply create a Shortcut to it. To do this right click anywhere on the desktop and select New > Shortcut. A new window titled Create Shortcut pops up. Type in the path of the restricted folder you wish to access, in this case c:\windows\system. Click Next, Enter the friendly name of the Shortcut and then click Finish. Now you can access the restricted folder by simply double clicking on the shortcut icon. Well that shows how protected and secure *ahem Windows *ahem is.

****

HACKING TRUTH: Sometimes when you try to delete a file or a folder, Windows displays an error message saying that the file is protected. This simply means that the file is write protected, or in other words the R option is +. Get it? Anyway, you can stop Windows from displaying this error message and straightaway delete this file by changing its attributes to Non Read Only. This can be done by Right Clicking on the file, selecting Properties and then

unselecting the Read Only Option.

****

There is yet another way of accessing restricted folders. Use see, DOS has a lovely command known as START. Its general syntax is:

START application_path

It does do what it seems to do, start applications. So in you have access to DOS then you can type in the START command to get access to the restricted folder. Now mostly access to DOS too would be blocked. So again you can use the shortcut trick to launch, c:\command.com or c:\windows\command.com. (Command.com is the file which launches MS DOS).

Accessing Restricted Drives.

The problem with most system administrators is that they think that the users or Hackers too are stupid. Almost all system administrators use the Registry

Trick (Explained Earlier) to hide all drives in My Computer. So in order to unhide or display all drives, simply delete that particular key.(Refer to beginning of Untold Secrets Section.)

Some systems have the floppy disk disabled through the BIOS. On those systems if the BIOS is protected, you may need to crack the BIOS password. (For that Refer to the Windows Hacking Chapter). Sometimes making drives readable (Removing R +) and then creating Shortcuts to them also helps us to get access to them.

Further Changing your Operating System's Looks by editing .htt files

If you have installed Windows Desktop Update and have the view as Web Page option enabled, you can customise the way the folder looks by selecting View > Customise this folder. Here you can change the background and other things about that particular folder. Well that is pretty lame, right? We hackers already know things as lame as that. Read on for some kewl stuff.

Well, you could also change the default that is stored in a Hidden HTML Template file (I think so..) which is nothing but a HTML document with a .htt extension. This .htt file is found at: %systemroot%\web\folder.htt.

The %systemroot% stands for the drive in which Windows is Installed, which is normally C:

You can edit these .htt files almost just like you edit normal .HTM or

.HTML files. Simply open them in an ASCII editor like Notepad. The following is a list of .htt files on your system which control various folders and which can be edited to customise the way various folders look.

controlp.htt Control Panel

printers.htt Printers

mycomp.htt My Computer

safemode.htt Safe Mode

All these files are found in the web folder in %systemfolder%. The folder.htt file has a line:

'Here's a good place to add a few lines of your own"

which is the place where you can add your own A HREF links. These links would then appear in the folder whose folder.htt file you edited. All this might sound really easy and simple, but you see these .htt files do not contain normal HTML code, instead they contain a mixture of HTML and web bots. Hence they can be difficult for newbies to understand.

Well that's it for now, more tricks later, till then goodbye.

_____

www.ingramcontent.com/pod-product-compliance
Lightning Source LLC
Chambersburg PA
CBHW071033050326
40689CB00014B/3636